USBORNE

FIRST THOUSAND WORDS

IN ENGLISH

Heather Amery

Illustrated by Stephen Cartwright

Edited by Nicole Irving
and designed by Andy Griffin

Hear the words on the internet

You can now listen to all the words in this book on the Usborne Quicklinks Website. Just go to **www.usborne-quicklinks.com** and enter the keywords **1000 english**. There you can:

- listen to the first thousand words

- find links to other useful websites for language learners about the English language, the USA and other English-speaking countries.

Note for parents and guardians

Please ensure that your children read and follow the internet safety guidelines displayed on the Usborne Quicklinks Website.

The links in Usborne Quicklinks are regularly reviewed and updated. However, the content of a website may change at any time, and Usborne Publishing is not responsible for the content on any website other than its own.

We recommend that children are supervised while on the internet, that they do not use internet chat rooms and that you use internet filtering software to block unsuitable material.

For more information, see the **Net Help** area on the Usborne Quicklinks Website.

On every big picture across two pages, there is a little yellow duck to look for. Can you find it?

About this book

All young children will enjoy this exciting picture word book. Parents and teachers sharing it with them will discover that each page provides lively situations to explore, and to talk and laugh about.

The First Thousand Words is designed to be used at many different levels, so that children of various ages and abilities will find it stimulating and amusing.

At its easiest level, the book can be used as a picture word book for looking and talking. As they grow familiar with favorite pages, children will be able to describe and give names to pictures. Gradually, they can be introduced to the printed words, and, with help and encouragement, they will soon begin matching words with pictures.

Older children can use this book when writing their own stories. It will provide them with ideas, new words and correct spellings.

There is a word list at the back of the book, which brings together all the words in alphabetical order. It can be used to encourage children to look up words and find the right page and picture. This is an important skill, which will prepare children to use simple information books and dictionaries.

Remember, this is a book of a thousand words. It will take time to learn them all!

About this revised edition

This edition brings new life to an enormously popular book. The book has been redesigned to give even clearer pictures and labels, and there are many brand-new illustrations by Stephen Cartwright. The book has also been brought up to date, so that it now includes objects which have made their way into children's everyday lives in recent years.

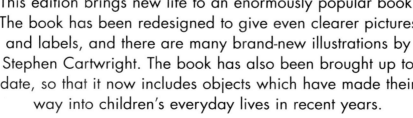

At home

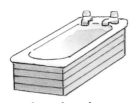
bathtub

soap

faucet

toilet paper

toothbrush

water

toilet

sponge

sink

shower

towel

bed

bathroom

living room

toothpaste

radio

cushion

CD

carpet

sofa

chair

comforter

comb

sheet

rug

closet

pillow

chest of drawers

mirror

brush

lamp

pictures

coat rack

telephone

bedroom

hall

radiator

video

newspaper

table

letters

stairs

5

refridgerator

glasses

clock

stool

teaspoons

switch

laundry
detergent

key

door

The kitchen

sink

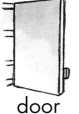

vacuum
cleaner

saucepans

forks

apron

ironing board

trash

kettle

 knives

mop

dust cloth

tiles

 broom

 washing machine

 dustpan

 drawer

 saucers

 frying pan

 stove

 spoons

 plates

 iron

 closet

 dish towel

 cups

 matches

 brush

 bowls

7

wheelbarrow

beehive

snail

bricks

pigeon

shovel

ladybug

trashcan

seeds

shed

The yard

watering can

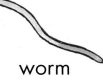

worm

flowers

sprinkler

hoe

wasp

8

bee

trowel

bone

hedge

fork

lawn mower

path

leaves

tree

smoke

caterpillar

rake

bird's nest

sticks

grass

baby buggy

ladder

bonfire

garden hose

greenhouse

9

The workshop

vice

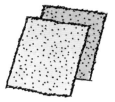
sandpaper

drill

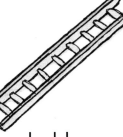
ladder

saw

sawdust

calendar

tool box

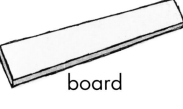
screwdriver

board

shavings

pocketknife

10

tacks

spider

bolts

nuts

cobweb

barrel

fly

ax

tape measure

hammer

file

paint can

wood

nails

workbench

jars

plane

11

The street

store

hole

café

ambulance

sidewalk

antenna

chimney

roof

bulldozer

hotel

bus

man

police car

pipes

drill

school

playground

12

taxi

crosswalk

factory

truck

traffic lights

movie theater

van

steamroller

trailer

house

market

steps

motorcycle

bicycle

fire engine

policeman

car

woman

lamp post

apartments

13

train set

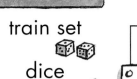

dice

The toyshop

harmonica

recorder

robot

drums

necklace

camera

beads

dolls

guitar

ring

doll's house

whistle   blocks   castle   submarine   trumpet   arrows

bow

parachute

boat

face paints

steamroller

masks

race car

rocking horse

bank

marbles

puppets

piano

spacemen

crane

clay

gun

soldiers

paints

rocket

15

swings

bench

The park

sandpit

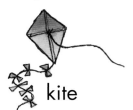
picnic

kite

ice cream

dog

gate

path

frog

slide

tadpoles

lake

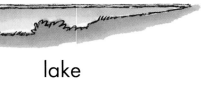
roller blades

bush

 **baby**

 **skateboard**

dirt

stroller

seesaw

 **children**

 tricycle

 birds

fence

 ball

 boat

 string

 puddle

 **ducklings**

 **jump-rope**

 **trees**

 **flower bed**

 **swans**

leash

 **ducks**

17

The zoo

panda

wing

eagle

hippopotamus

bat

monkey

tail

gorilla

paws

kangaroo

iceberg

penguin

wolf

crocodile

bear

feathers

pelican

ostrich

dolphin

lion

cubs

giraffe

18

antlers

deer

camel

seal

polar bear

tortoise

trunk

rhinoceros

bison

elephant

beaver

goat

zebra

snake

shark

whale

tiger

leopard

19

Travel

helicopter

train track

engine

buffers

railway cars

engineer

freight train

platform

conductor

suitcase

ticket machine

The railway station

The garage

signals

backpack

headlights

engine

wheel

battery

20

The airport

plane

flight attendant

runway

control tower

flight attendant

pilot

car wash

trunk

gas

tow truck

car wash

tanker

wrench

tire

hood

oil

gas pump

21

The country

windmill

hot-air balloon

butterfly

lizard

stones

fox

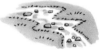
stream

signpost

porcupine

lock

mountain

squirrel

forest

badger

river

road

22

tents

canal

logs

town

moth

bridge

barge

waterfall

owl

tunnel

fox cubs

mole

fisherman

rocks

toad

train

camper

hill

haystack

sheepdog

ducks

lambs

pond

chicks

hayloft

pigsty

bull

ducklings

hen house

tractor

The farm

rooster

geese

tanker

barn

mud

cart

24

farmer

field

hens

calf

fence

saddle

cowshed

cow

plow

orchard

stable

piglets

shepherdess

turkeys

scarecrow

farmhouse

hay

sheep

straw bales

horse

pigs

The seaside

sailboat

sea

oar

lighthouse

shovel

bucket

starfish

sandcastle

umbrella

flag

sailor

shell

crab

seagull

island

motor-boat

water-skier

waves

sunhat

cliff

ship

kayak

rope

pebbles

seaweed

net

paddle

fishing boat

flippers

donkey

fish

swimsuit

oil tanker

beach

rowboat

beach chair

27

scissors

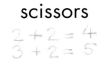

sums

eraser

ruler

photographs

felt-tip pens

thumbtacks

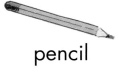

paints

boy

At school

board

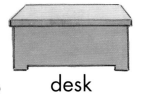

desk

books

pen

glue

chalk

drawing

pencil

28

wastepaper basket

teacher

box

map

brush

ceiling

wall

floor

notebook

alphabet

badge

aquarium

paper

blind

a b c d e f g
h i j k l m n
o p q r s t u
v w x y z

door handle

plant

globe

girl

crayons

lamp

easel

The hospital

nurse

cotton balls

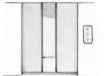
medicine

elevator

bathrobe

crutches

pills

tray

watch

thermometer

curtain

teddy bear

apple

cast

bandage

wheelchair

jigsaw

doctor

syringe

The doctor

slippers

computer

adhesive bandage

banana

grapes

basket

toys

pear

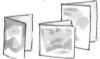
cards

diaper

walking stick

waiting room

television

nightgown

pajamas

orange

tissues

comic

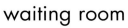

31

balloon

The party

chocolate

candy

window

fireworks

ribbon

cake

straw

candle

paper chains

toys

tangerine

salami

cassette tape

sausage

chips

costumes

cherry

fruit juice

raspberry

strawberry

bulb

sandwich

butter

cookie

cheese

bread

tablecloth

33

The store

grapefruit

carrot

cauliflower

leek

mushroom

cucumber

lemon

celery

apricot

melon

grocery sack

CHEESE

FRUIT AND VEGETABLES

onion

cabbage

peach

lettuce

peas

tomato

eggs

 plum

 flour

 scales

jars

 meat

 pineapple

 yogurt

basket

 bottles

 purse

coin purse

 money

 cans

 cart

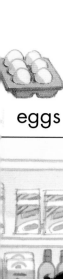

 potatoes

 spinach

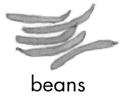 beans

 checkout

 pumpkin

 cart

35

Food

breakfast

lunch or dinner

boiled egg

toast

jam

coffee

fried egg

cream

milk

cereal

hot chocolate

sugar

honey

salt

pepper

tea

teapot

pancakes

rolls

supper or dinner

ham

soup

omelette

salad

chopsticks

hamburger

chicken

rice

ketchup

spaghetti

mashed potatoes

pizza

french fries

dessert

37

Me

head — hair — face

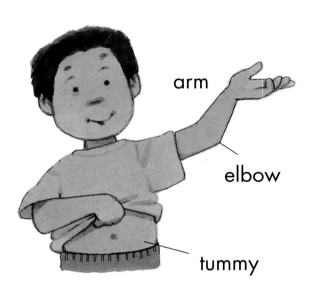
arm — elbow — tummy

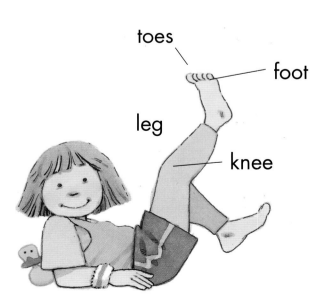
toes — foot — leg — knee

eyebrow

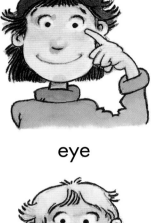
eye

nose

cheek

mouth

lips

teeth

tongue

chin

ears

neck

shoulders

chest

back

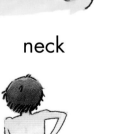
bottom

hand

thumb

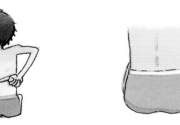
fingers

My clothes

socks

underwear

undershirt

pants

jeans

T-shirt

skirt

shirt

tie

shorts

tights

dress

sweater

sweatshirt

cardigan

scarf

handkerchief

tennis shoes

shoes

sandals

boots

gloves

belt

buckle

zipper

shoelace

buttons

button holes

pockets

coat

jacket

cap

hat

People

actor

actress

chef

dancers

singers

butcher

policeman

policewoman

astronaut

carpenter

fireman

artist

judge

mechanics

truck driver

bus driver

barber

dentist

frogman

mail carrier

painter

baker

waiter   waitress

Families

aunt   uncle

grandfather

son   daughter   mother   father
brother   sister   wife   husband

cousin

grandmother

Doing things

laugh

smile

cry

think

listen

catch

throw

break

paint

write

chop

cut

eat

talk

dig

carry

drink

make

jump

crawl

dance

wash

knit

play

watch

climb

fight

sleep

take

sew

skip

wait

cook

hide

read

buy

push

sweep

sing

pick

blow

pull

fall

walk

run

sit

43

Opposite words

good

bad

far

near

cold

hot

wet

dry

top

bottom

over

under

dirty

clean

fat

thin

open

closed

small

big

few

many

first

last

left

out

in

easy

difficult

empty

full

soft

hard

front

high

slow

fast

back

low

long

short

dead

alive

dark

light

old

upstairs

right

new

downstairs

45

Days

Monday
Tuesday
Wednesday
Thursday
Friday
Saturday
Sunday

calendar

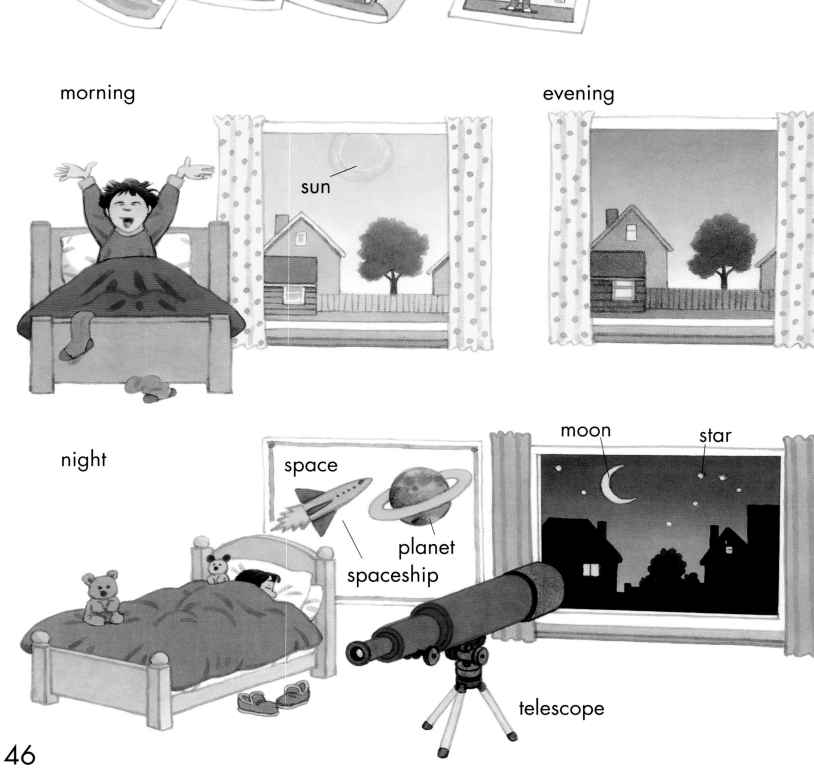

morning

sun

evening

night

space

moon

star

planet

spaceship

telescope

Special days

birthday

birthday card

candle

present

birthday cake

vacation

wedding day

bridesmaid

bride bridegroom

camera

photographer

Christmas day

reindeer

sleigh

Santa Claus

Christmas tree

47

Weather

sun

clouds

sky

umbrella

rain

lightning

fog

snow

dew

wind

mist

frost

rainbow

Seasons

spring

summer

fall

winter

48

Pets

vet

hamster

guinea pig

kennel

puppy

dog

parakeet

food

parrot

beak

rabbit

canary

cage

cat

basket

mouse

kitten

milk

goldfish

49

Sport and exercise

basketball

rowing

sailing

windsurfing

snowboarding

racket

tennis

football

gym

cricket

karate

bat

ball

fishing rod

fishing

bait

rugby

dance

baseball

diving

swimming pool

race

swimming

archery

target

hang-gliding

jogging

cycling

helmet

climbing

judo

horse

pony

locker

soccer

changing room

riding

badminton

ice skates

table tennis

ice-skating

ski pole

chairlift

ski

skiing

sumo wrestling

51

Colors

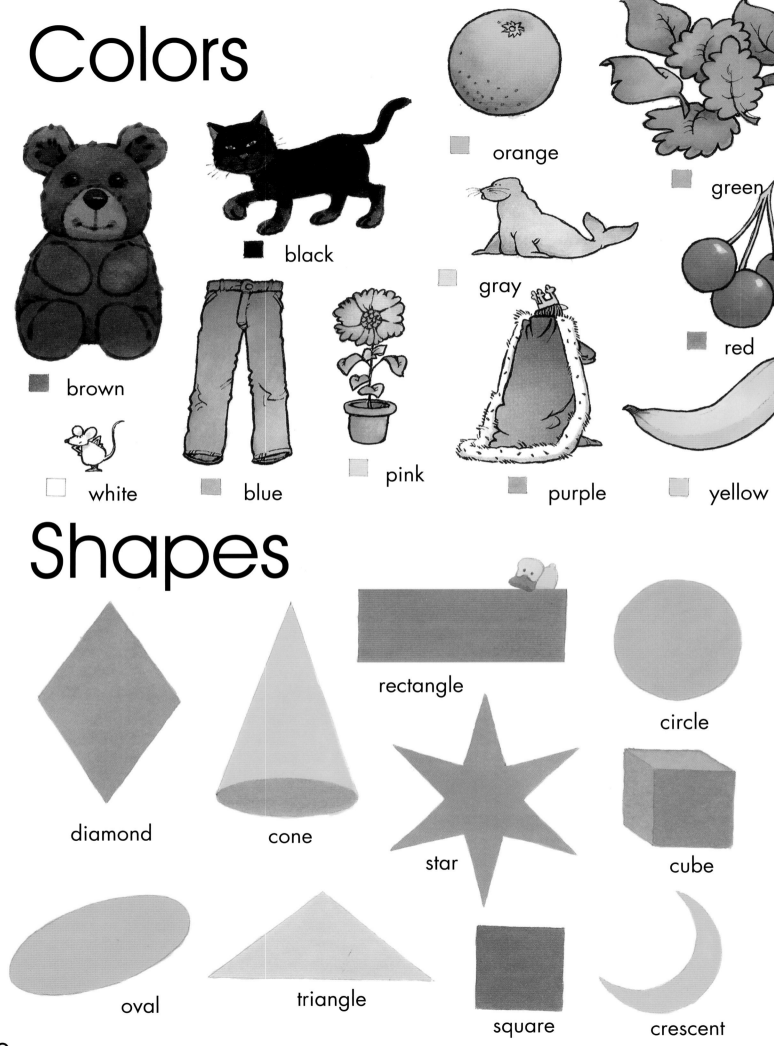

orange

green

black

gray

red

brown

pink

white blue purple yellow

Shapes

rectangle

circle

diamond cone

star

cube

oval triangle square crescent

Numbers

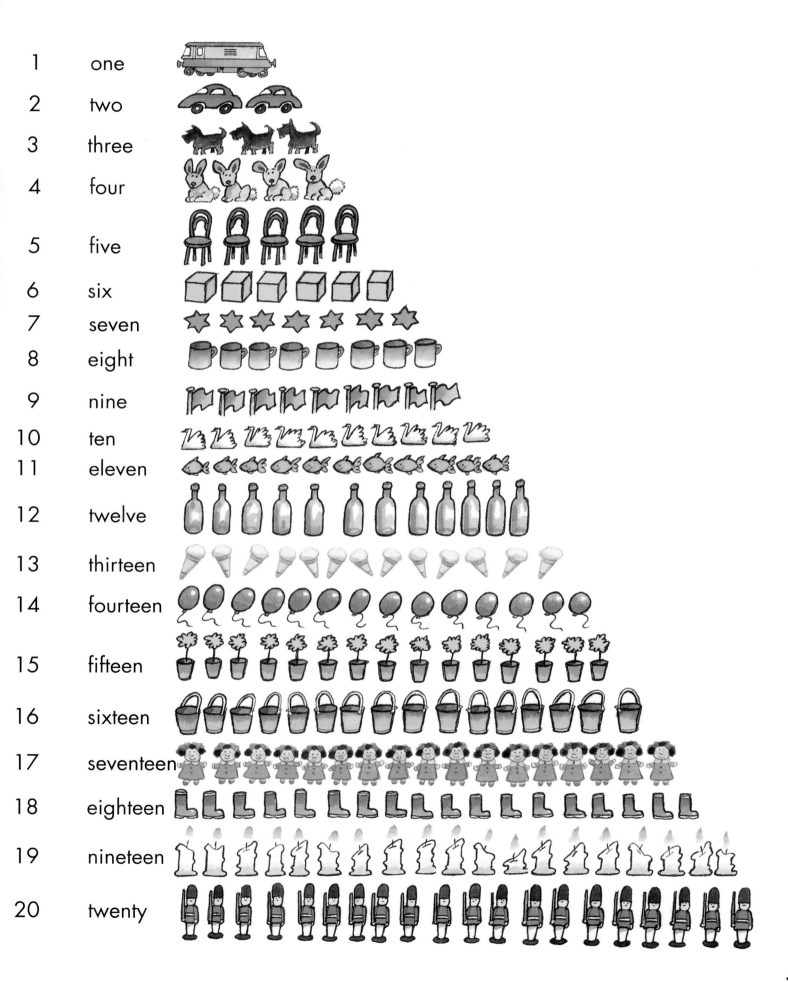

1	one
2	two
3	three
4	four
5	five
6	six
7	seven
8	eight
9	nine
10	ten
11	eleven
12	twelve
13	thirteen
14	fourteen
15	fifteen
16	sixteen
17	seventeen
18	eighteen
19	nineteen
20	twenty

Amusement Park

merry-go-round

mat

slide

Ferris wheel

amusement ride

popcorn

ring toss

roller coaster

rifle range

bumper cars

cotton candy

Circus

unicyclist

trapeze

tightrope walker

pole

tightrope

rope ladder

safety net

acrobats

rabbit

ring master

dog

top hat

juggler

hoop

bow tie

band

bareback rider

clown

Words in order

This is a list of all the words in the picture pages. They are in the same order as the alphabet. After each word is a page number. On that page, you will find the word and picture together.

a

acrobats, 55
actor, 40
actress, 40
adhesive bandage, 31
airport, 21
alive, 45
alphabet, 29
ambulance, 12
amusement park, 54
amusement ride, 54
antenna, 12
antlers, 19
apartments, 13
apple, 30
apricot, 34
apron, 6
aquarium, 29
archery, 51
arm, 38
arrows, 14
artist, 40
astronaut, 40
aunt, 41
ax, 11

b

baby, 17
baby buggy, 9
back (of body), 38
back (not front), 45
backpack, 20

bad, 44
badge, 29
badger, 22
badminton, 51
bait, 50
baker, 41
ball, 17, 50
balloon, 32
banana, 31
band, 55
bandage, 30
bank, 15
barber, 41
bareback rider, 55
barge, 23
barn, 24
barrel, 11
baseball, 50
basket, 31, 35, 49
basketball, 50
bat (animal), 18
bat (for sports), 50
bathrobe, 30
bathtub, 4
bathroom, 4
battery, 20
beach, 27
beach chair, 27
beads, 14
beak, 49
beans, 35
bear, 18, 19, 30
beaver, 19
bed, 4
bedroom, 5
bee, 9
beehive, 8
belt, 39
bench, 16
bicycle, 13
big, 44
birds, 17
bird's nest, 9
birthday, 47
birthday cake, 47

birthday card, 47
bison, 19
black, 52
blind (for a window), 29
blocks, 14
blow, 43
blue, 52
board, 10, 28
boat, 15, 17, 26, 27
boiled egg, 36
bolts, 11
bone, 9
bonfire, 9
books, 28
boots, 39
bottles, 35
bottom (of body), 38
bottom (not top), 44
bow, 15
bowls, 7
bow tie, 55
box, 29
boy, 28
bread, 33
break, 42
breakfast, 36
bricks, 8
bride, 47
bridegroom, 47
bridesmaid, 47
bridge, 23
broom, 7
brother, 41
brown, 52
brush, 5, 7, 29
bucket, 26
buckle, 39
buffers (train), 20
bulb (light), 33
bull, 24
bulldozer, 12
bumper cars, 54
bus, 12
bus driver, 41
bush, 16

dice, 14
difficult, 45
dig, 42
dinner, 36, 37
dirt, 17
dirty, 44
dish towel, 7
diving, 50
doctor, 30, 31
dog, 16, 49, 55
doing things, 42
dolls, 14
doll's house, 14
dolphin, 18
donkey, 27
door, 6
door handle, 29
downstairs, 45
drawer, 7
drawing, 28
dress, 39
drill, 10, 12
drink, 42
drums, 14
dry, 44
ducklings, 17, 24
ducks, 17, 24
dust cloth, 7
dustpan, 7

e

eagle, 18
ears, 38
easel, 29
easy, 45
eat, 42
egg, 36
eggs, 35
eight, 53
eighteen, 53
elbow, 38
elephant, 19
elevator, 30
eleven, 53
empty, 45

engine, 20
engineer, 20
eraser, 28
evening, 46
exercise, 50
eye, 38
eyebrow, 38

f

face, 38
face paints, 15
factory, 13
fall, 43
fall (season), 48
families, 41
far, 44
farm, 24
farmer, 25
farmhouse, 25
fast, 45
fat, 44
father, 41
faucet, 4
feathers, 18
felt-tip pens, 28
fence, 17, 25
ferris wheel, 54
few, 44
field, 25
fifteen, 53
fight, 43
flight attendant, 21
file, 11
fingers, 38
fire engine, 13
fireman, 40
fireworks, 32
first, 44
fish, 27
fisherman, 23
fishing, 50
fishing boat, 27
fishing rod, 50
five, 53
flag, 26

flippers, 27
floor, 29
flour, 35
flower bed, 17
flowers, 8
fly, 11
fog, 48
food, 36, 49
foot, 38
football, 50
forest, 22
fork (garden), 9
forks, 6
four, 53
fourteen, 53
fox, 22
fox cubs, 23
freight train, 20
french fries, 37
Friday, 46
fried egg, 36
frog, 16
frogman, 41
front, 45
frost, 48
fruit, 34
fruit juice, 33
frying pan, 7
full, 45

g

garage, 20
garden hose, 9
gas, 21
gas pump, 21
gate, 16
geese, 24
giraffe, 18
girl, 29
glasses (for drinking), 6
globe, 29
gloves, 39
glue, 28
goat, 19
goldfish, 49

good, 44
gorilla, 18
grandfather, 41
grandmother, 41
grapefruit, 34
grapes, 31
grass, 9
gray, 52
green, 52
greenhouse, 9
grocery bag, 34
guinea pig, 49
guitar, 14
gun, 15
gym, 50

h

hair, 38
hall, 5
ham, 37
hamburger, 37
hammer, 11
hamster, 49
hand, 38
handkerchief, 39
hang-gliding, 51
hard, 45
harmonica, 14
hat, 39
hay, 25
hayloft, 24
haystack, 24
head, 38
headlights, 20
hedge, 9
helicopter, 20
helmet, 51
hen house, 24
hens, 25
hide, 43
high, 45
hill, 23
hippopotamus, 18
hoe, 8
hole, 12

home, 4
honey, 36
hood (of a car), 21
hoop, 55
horse, 25, 51
hospital, 30
hot, 44
hot-air balloon, 22
hot chocolate, 36
hotel, 12
house, 13
husband, 41

i

iceberg, 18
ice cream, 16
ice skates, 51
ice-skating, 51
in, 45
iron, 7
ironing board, 6
island, 26

j

jacket, 39
jam, 36
jars, 11, 35
jeans, 39
jigsaw, 30
jogging, 51
judge, 40
judo, 51
juggler, 55
jump, 42
jump-rope, 17

k

kangaroo, 18
karate, 50
kayak, 27
kennel, 49
ketchup, 37
kettle, 7

key, 6
kitchen, 6
kite, 16
kitten, 49
knee, 38
knit, 42
knives, 7

l

ladder, 9, 10
ladybug, 8
lake, 16
lambs, 24
lamp, 5, 29
lamp post, 13
last, 44
laugh, 42
laundry detergent, 6
lawn mower, 9
leash, 17
leaves, 9
leek, 34
left, 44
leg, 38
lemon, 34
leopard, 19
letters, 5
lettuce, 34
light, 45
lighthouse, 26
lightning, 48
light switch, 6
lion, 18
lips, 38
listen, 42
living room, 4
lizard, 22
lock, 22
locker, 51
logs, 23
long, 45
low, 45
lunch, 36

m

mail carrier, 41
make, 42
man, 12
many, 44
map, 29
marbles, 15
market, 13
mashed potatoes, 37
masks, 15
mat, 54
matches, 7
me, 38
meat, 35
mechanics, 40
medicine, 30
melon, 34
merry-go-round, 54
milk, 36, 49
mirror, 5
mist, 48
mole, 23
Monday, 46
money, 35
monkey, 18
moon, 46
mop, 7
morning, 46
moth, 23
mother, 41
motorboat, 26
motorcycle, 13
mountain, 22
mouse, 49
mouth, 38
movie theater, 13
mud, 24
mushroom, 34
my, 39

n

nails, 11
near, 44
neck, 38
necklace, 14
net, 27
new, 45
newspaper, 5
night, 46
nightgown, 31
nine, 53
nineteen, 53
nose, 38
notebook, 29
numbers, 53
nurse, 30
nuts, 11

o

oar, 26
oil, 21
oil tanker, 27
old, 45
omelette, 37
one, 53
onion, 34
open, 44
opposite words, 44
orange (colour), 52
orange (fruit), 31
orchard, 25
ostrich, 18
out, 45
oval, 52
over, 44
owl, 23

p

paddle, 27
paint, 42
paint can, 11
painter, 41
paints, 15, 28
pajamas, 31
pancakes, 36
panda, 18
pants, 39
paper, 29
paper chains, 32
parachute, 15
parakeet, 49
park, 16
parrot, 49
party, 32
path, 9, 16
pavement, 12
paws, 18
peach, 34
pear, 31
peas, 34
pebbles, 27
pelican, 18
pen, 28
pencil, 28
penguin, 18
people, 40
pepper, 36
pets, 49
photographer, 47
photographs, 28
piano, 15
pick, 43
picnic, 16
pictures, 5
pigeon, 8
piglets, 25
pigs, 25
pigsty, 24
pillow, 5
pills, 30
pilot, 21
pineapple, 35
pink, 52
pipes, 12
pizza, 37
plane, 11, 21
planet, 46
plant, 29
plates, 7
platform, 20
play, 43
playground, 12
plow, 25
plum, 35

This revised edition first published in 2010 by Usborne Publishing Ltd, Usborne House, 83-85 Saffron Hill, London EC1N 8RT, England. www.usborne.com

Copyright © 2010, 1995, 1979 Usborne Publishing Ltd.
First published in America in 2010

The name Usborne and the devices are Trade Marks of Usborne Publishing Ltd. All rights reserved.